20 Questions to Consider If Business (FRANCHISE) Ownership Is Right For You?

Copyright © 2016 by Ken Boyce.

All rights reserved.

No part of this book may be reproduced in any form or by any electronic or mechanical means including information storage and retrieval systems, without permission in writing from the author. The only exception is by a reviewer, who may quote short excerpts in a review.

Disclaimer of Liability

Although the author has made every effort to ensure that the information in this book was correct at press time, the author and publisher do not assume and hereby disclaim any liability to any party for any loss, damage, or disruption caused by errors or omissions, whether such errors or omissions result from negligence, accident, or any other cause. All information is provided as points of view. Always hire a professional advisor before purchasing a business.

Printed in the United States of America

First Printing: September 2016

ISBN-10: 1537770284
ISBN-13: 978-1537770284

Table of Contents

Introduction	3
About The Author	4
Question #1 – "Is Opening A Business Too Risky?"	9
Question #2 – "Is It True That Most Businesses Fail?"	11
Question #3 – "Don't I Need An MBA or Business Degree?"	13
Question #4 – "Why Should I Pay A Franchise Fee? I Can Just Do It Myself..	15
Question #5 – "Why Leave The Security of My Job?"	17
Question #6 – " I Am Not Sure If I Can Work On My Own?"..	19
Question #7 – "Why The Lack Of Support?" The Naysayers!	21
Question #8 – "How Do I Know This Business Is Right For Me?	23
Question #9 – Do I Have The Necessary Capital to Open A Business?	25
Question #10 – "I Hear Business Owners Pay Less Taxes. Is That True?"	27
Question #11 – "Do I Need Experience In The Industry?"	29
Question #12 – Is It Wise To Have Family Members In My Business?	31
Question #13 – "Is It OK To Have A Business Partner?"	33
Question #14 – "How Should I Structure My Business?"	36
Question #15 – "Is Owning A Business Better Than Working In Corporate America?"	39
Question #16 – "Which Industries Have the Best Opportunity?"	41
Question #17 – "Should I Purchase An Existing or Start-up Business?"	43
Question #18 – "How Do I Perform Due Diligence On A Business?"	45
Question #19 – "How Long Will It Take To Make Money?" ...	47
Question #20 – Use Retirement Funds To Fund A Business?	50

Introduction

Am I biased on business ownership? ABSOLUTELY! It has been my professional life for the past 20 years. The main reason, I am biased, is due to the tremendous amount of success that my clients, friends, and colleagues have accomplished.

Does that mean you should be self-employed? I never tell people that they should become a business owner. This book is meant to help you raise questions and self-reflect to help determine if business ownership is meant for you.

Here are the 20 most commonly asked questions I have heard over the years from individuals looking at the possibility of business or franchise ownership.

I will also help define the differences of owning a franchise business over owning an independent business.

The clients I have worked with are looking to make a change for themselves and their family. It is a very serious change. They want to be sure to make the right choice. Failure is not an option.

This book is meant for individuals who are seriously thinking about taking their future into their own hands. It will be helpful whether you may have just started thinking about being in your own business or have already determined you want to be self-employed.

I hope you enjoy the book. These questions are put together to help paint a picture for you from the beginning of a person's journey of potential business ownership.

I share conversations and experiences that many hundreds of individuals searching for business ownership have shared with me. If you ever become a business owner, you will understand that the entrepreneur club is a humble, strong, private, giving, rewarding club. I always consider it to be a privilege to be part of it.

I wish you the best of luck on your journey to success.

ABOUT THE AUTHOR

Born in a small town in Nova Scotia, Canada, I grew up in a blue collar family and neighborhood. I had a very normal childhood that was centered around sports, education, and parents who always gave me enough rope to hang myself to learn from my mistakes.

I played many competitive sports but excelled in one...Golf. After having a very successful junior career in Canada, I needed to decide what to pursue. Golf or Education? In 1986, professional golfers were not playing for $1,000,000 per tournament but I decided to enter a few minor professional tournaments in Florida. Sleeping in my car, showering in the clubhouse, learning that most of my competitors played golf year round (Golf season in Nova Scotia is 5 months at best) and more importantly, not winning any money, made my decision very easy!

University it is! I completed my Bachelor of Commerce degree and decided to work in the golf industry. I started as an assistant golf pro at a private club in Halifax, Nova Scotia. Be careful making your hobby or passion into a business. I found out that playing golf and working in the golf industry are two different things. Sitting behind the counter in the pro shop and teaching people how to swing a club was not burning any fire in my belly.

One day a member of the club said to me, "Looks like you lost your best friend" I replied, "No...just going through a career dilemma." That member was Bruce Reardon and he was the general manager of a large insurance company. Bruce said "Come talk to me about selling life insurance and financial services. I am sure that is exactly what you were thinking about!" I laughed to myself. Life insurance? Yeah...right! Like I wanted to do that! Before saying anything to Bruce I took a moment to reflect on Bruce's lifestyle. "He drives a very nice car, lives in one of the nicest neighborhoods in the area, plays golf 4 times a week. Hold on... Sure sounds like a lifestyle I would like to have!" I accepted Bruce's invitation to meet him at his office and learn more.

Moving two years forward, I earned the top rookie award for the company for all of Canada. After two years of tremendous success and dedication, working all the time was catching up to me. All work and no play was now no fun! I sat down with Bruce and told him how I was feeling. Bruce acknowledges, "It took me 15 years to get where I am today. I know you are a hard worker. You should be able to get where I am in that same time period." Bruce saw me turn white and broke the tension with his large infectious laugh. **This was one of the most pivotal moments in my professional life.** Bruce came over to where I was sitting and pulled up a chair. Bruce puts his hand on my shoulder and says, "It is time for you to go." I look at Bruce with shock, "You are firing me?"

"No...I am setting you free!" I thought that Bruce had lost his mind. Bruce continues, "I have had the pleasure to be part of your journey. I remember seeing you in the golf pro shop almost every day and how well you treated people, organized the shop and thinking about others before yourself. I knew you were a leader. You just didn't know it. I have always subscribed to helping people become the best that they can be. You are welcome to stay with us as long as you wish. I want you to relax, take your time and think about our conversation. I have been an entrepreneur for the past 20 years. I own other businesses, as you are aware, and think you would make a great entrepreneur. Whatever you decide, you have my full support!" My jaw dropped. I was speechless.

I took Bruce's advise. Over the next 5 years, I started a small telecommunications service and opened an Information Technology recruiting business. I had moderate success. The challenge was learning along the way. Every time I took one step forward, I felt like I was paying for my lack of experience, and taking two steps back. I realized that my lack of life experience was preventing me to excel forward.

I decided to move to Toronto, Canada. The big city! Looking to make that next step in my career, I fell into an opportunity to sell franchises for a home inspection company.

Franchise companies always intrigued me. I knew a couple of individuals that owned a Subway and a McDonalds. What I did not realize was how many franchise companies existed. (Today there are over 3,500 different franchise companies in business.) For the next 5 years, I learned a tremendous amount about the franchise industry and help grow the company from 35 franchise owners to over 300 franchise owners. Most of the locations opened in the U.S.

I was on a real high and one day a franchise candidate asked me, "Have you ever thought about owning a franchise business?" What a great question! The answer was actually no. I was having great success that it just never occurred to me. WOW! What a question. **This was another pivotal moment in my life.** Can I be in my own business again? I already understood that owning a franchise is purchasing a proven business model. Many of the current franchise owners never had any home inspection experience. What they all had in common was the desire to take control of their own destiny.

Later that same month, I was attending a franchise convention and started looking at many of the franchise companies who were looking for new franchise owners. The first thing that came to mind was...look how many companies are here! Where do I start? What companies are best for me? I then saw one of my colleagues that I have known for 5 years and he was representing an automotive franchise. I stopped to say hello and asked him when he started with this company. He said, "Ken, I own the company." I congratulated him and we started to talk about the business. He said that they wanted to expand into Canada and if I would be interested in helping develop franchises. My response was, "How about actually opening a location in Toronto?" This lead to the next stage in my career. For the next 4 years, I built up a successful business which was eventually sold to one of my competitors.

What next? I already knew what I wanted to do next. One of the most respected individuals in franchising asked me to join his firm. Kurt owned a franchise development company. He helped emerging franchise companies grow their brands across the country.

Kurt asked me to work with him, as he had more clients than he could handle.

For the next 5 years, we worked with many franchise companies and helped to put over 500 people into their own franchised business. It was an incredible experience! The opportunity allowed me to meet so many successful franchise professionals and become part of the franchise community.

I have now been in the franchise industry for over 20 years and have learned an incredible amount from the professionals in the industry. I made a point to always sit with the CEO's at franchise conventions and learn as much as I could. Utilizing those relationships and my previous experience allowed me to grow and put myself in a position to finally become a franchisor. It was important to me to utilize what I had learned and progress in my career. I searched for an industry and company that I felt had great potential. I identified a number of companies but one shined through. For the next 4 years, I dedicated my energy in building a salon suite company. The company grew to 40 franchise owners with 25 locations open and operating. A larger company fell in love with our business and reached out to become a partner. This was a great addition to help our current franchise owners grow and open more locations. After further negotiations, I was able to benefit from all of the efforts and sell my shares in the company. It was time that I focused on what was most important in my life. My family.

I currently have been married for 13 years. This is my daughter's lucky number! Shannon is 9 years old and probably the most perfect daughter in the world! Shannon inspires me to be a better person every day. Her kindred spirit, love for other people and beyond cuteness come from my better half, Paula. My wife is incredibly beautiful, smart and keeps me grounded. She is the rock in our relationship that allows me to be the best I can be. That is the reason I have decided to be incredibly selfish. I want to spend as much time with my family as possible.

The current stage in my professional career is a professional franchise consultant. I now have an office in Sarasota, Florida and help individuals looking to make the transition from Corporate America to franchise ownership. My clients may be looking to leave Corporate America or find a franchise opportunity that allows them to keep their current positions. They leverage my experience, knowledge, and REAL LIFE expertise to help guide them into the next phase of their lives. It is incredibly important to me to help people make the right choices for the right reasons.

Question #1 – "Is Opening A Business Too Risky?"

This is one of the most common question that I have heard from clients over the years. There are many times that a business is too risky and would not be the best option. Based on U.S. Bureau of Labor Statistics 2015 data, an estimated 16 million individuals own a business. I have seen other sources that the number is as high as 30 million people. It depends on who you are counting. For the sake of argument, let's just say it is between 5-10% of individuals will actually be self-employed. It is still a small percentage. Let's explore the reasons why business owners typically fail. The Harvard Entrepreneurship wrote an article in 2016 that described the top 10 reasons why a business fails.

Here are the 10 reasons:

- No Written Business Plan
- No Projected Revenue
- A Good Idea Is Not Always Good Business
- Lack of Execution
- Too Much Competition
- No Intellectual Property
- Inexperienced Team
- Underestimated Resources
- Inefficient Marketing
- Giving Up Too Early

The reason why most people say that a business is too risky is a lack of preparation and execution. Answer this question:

"What happens in your current position if you do not produce?"

The answer I usually get from most individuals is they either get demoted or even lose their job. Think of it another way. How is a business any riskier than starting a new job? Would you rather have complete control of your success or be in a situation where other people in the organization affect your future?

Have you been in a department that other individuals are having an effect on the ability to do your job but have no control to do anything about it? This is one of the major factors that push people into self-employment.

The term self-employment is a great alternative to business ownership. Just because you own a business does not mean that you do not work. What it means is you work for yourself. I know many business owners that work very hard to be successful. I will share with you that if you own a business that no one will care more about the success of the business then you will.

So let me ask you this question?

Is there more risk in working for someone else compared to working for yourself?

The answer is up to you. If you are thinking self-employment is for you, I suggest you consider the term "Calculated Risk". Many business owners use this term.

In other words, those who are properly prepared reduce the risk of failure. We will discuss later how a franchise business dramatically reduces the risk of failure.

Here is my favorite quote on risk:

"In the end, we only regret the chances we did not take".
– Unknown.

Question #2 – "Is It True That Most Businesses Fail?"

This is an excellent question! Let's first look at the statistics. The SBA (Small Business Administration) is the leading government resource on small business. The SBA evaluates that 50% of businesses fail within the first 5 years. The statistics say you have a 50/50 chance to be successful. Do you think that is good or bad? When I heard the stats I was surprised that it was that low. My assumption was the percentage of failures would be higher.

If I told you that you had a 50/50 chance of having a successful business would you take the challenge? What if there was a way to increase the chances of success? The U.S. Department of Commerce did a survey and published that their findings indicated that 95% of franchise-based companies were still in business after 5 years. Wow! That is amazing!

Hold on. The IFA (International Franchise Association) has come out and debated the validity of those findings. The IFA does not believe that number is accurate. They believe it is lower. The numbers are incredibly hard to determine. There are over 3,500 franchise organizations in over 80 industries. The difficulty in tracking the numbers are due to the differences in the maturity of the franchise companies, the amount of investment and other factors. I would suggest you take all these stats with a grain of salt. These are the facts. You need to evaluate them and come up with your own conclusions.

The one figure that is accurate is 50% of businesses are still open after 5 years. In my humble opinion, having a proven franchise system should greatly increase your chance to success.

You now know the facts. It is up to you to decide if they make you feel better or worse. I would suggest that you try to increase your percentage of success. How do you do that? Start by referring back to the top 10 reasons why businesses fail. We will also discuss more suggestions to increase your chance of success later on.

There is one characteristic that I have found that is overwhelmingly prevalent in entrepreneurs. **Optimism**. They look at their business through a glass half full instead of half empty.

I have worked with many people, who look at the option of self-employment, but only looked at what was wrong instead of what was right. My suggestion is always to take a balanced approached. The power of positive thought is a powerful tool.

My favorite quote on failure is:

"Most great people have their greatest success just one step beyond their greatest failure. - Napoleon Hill

Question #3 – "Don't I Need an MBA or Business Degree?"

There are many entrepreneurs and self-employed individuals that hold business degrees or an MBA. These are fantastic credentials to acquire that will help you to effectively operate a business. Knowledge is power and the more equipped you are, the greater you increase your chance of success.

I have also met many entrepreneurs and self-employed individuals that have far less education. In fact, there is one colleague that I know that only has a grade 6 education and built a multi-million dollar empire. His story is an amazing one. His father was killed when he was 12 years old. In order for his family to survive, he had to go to work. He had to lie about his age and got his first job in a manufacturing factory. He was able to make enough money to help put food on the table but needed to make more. He started his first business delivering newspapers. He soon was given his own route area. His success derived from the necessity to live. If you asked him today, he would tell you that he has an MBA from the school of Hard Knox.

I have met many people without the formal education that have a great desire to take control of their own lives. Unfortunately, many of them do not have the experience, knowledge or expertise to run a successful business. I always say give me a person with a burning desire to succeed above anything else. It is far easier to teach and support an individual. Franchise Companies are ideal for these type of individuals, as they already have a proven business model. All you have to do is follow the plan.

Franchise companies are looking for the best-qualified candidates to represent them in an area. The key factor that they assess in a potential new owner is attitude and the ability to be teachable. Being part of a franchise is learning a new industry and systems. The franchise companies have already built systems and processes based on their experience. They typically are looking for people to follow these systems and processes because they work.

In fact, many of the franchise companies build a profile or model that is based on their successful owners.

They know exactly the type of person will do well in their business. That is a major factor why franchises have a higher success rate than operators of independently owned businesses.

Companies build a job description for a position in their company. Quality franchise companies will not award a franchise to a person unless they possess the necessary skill sets that match their criteria.

Just like many other industries you have the small percentage that are not professional. In the franchise industry we call these companies "Churn and Burn" companies. If you are breathing and have money they will welcome you in. If you are not successful they will just award your franchise to someone else. Beware of these companies!!! You can avoid these companies by performing the proper due diligence. You have the ultimate decision to say yes or no. Working with a franchise consultant can help you avoid these types of companies all together. Just make sure that franchise consultant is professionally qualified.

Having an MBA or higher level of education is a positive. If you do not have the formal education I would like to have you think about this quote and hope it helps you.

"Education is not the learning of facts. It's the training of the mind to think." – Albert Einstein.

Question #4 – "Why Should I Pay a Franchise Fee? I Can Just Do It Myself."

I do not know anyone that is excited about having to write a check to a franchise company. Why not just start my business as an independent? I can keep these funds and put it towards my own brand. This is definitely a choice. Let's dive a little deeper into the reason behind why franchise companies charge an initial franchise fee and an ongoing royalty fee.

Whether you decide to open an independent or franchise business, you need to agree and understand that all companies need to make revenue to survive and be successful. It is amazing to me how many people have not given this premise more thought. I can guarantee if you decide to be self-employed that you will understand.

What you need to be asking is what value do I receive? If you spend money on an education, the value is opening doors to a better job. If you spend money on a 401k, the value is saving for retirement. If you purchase a franchise, you are spending money to acquire a proven business model. The key to understand is you are not really spending money. You are investing in yourself and want to make the best choices that produce the best results.

Let's look at the differences between opening an independent business and a franchise business. Let's start with an independent business. Starting a business is going to require you to invest money. You will have to design a logo, build a website, purchase equipment and supplies, hire employees, spend money on marketing and many more items just to get started. You will have to find companies to help you and figure out which companies are the best. This can take a lot of time and hopefully you do not make many mistakes that cost you too much money.

A franchise business is a turn-key business. All of the things that you need to do to get started are already completed. Most importantly, you may be purchasing version 5.3. Franchise companies are always upgrading their business model. You benefit from all their years of experience. Compare it to a University degree. How much would you spend to gain the knowledge of a University degree in one day? Now consider the time and energy you would save?

Recently, one of my clients made a comment that he spent $200,000 on his daughters' education and she cannot get a job. His comment was, "Maybe it would of been better to buy my daughter a business."

Current franchise owners understand the value. It does not mean that a franchise system is right for every business or for every person. It really comes down to reducing time and risk. A franchise system will provide this to you.

These are all suggestions to help you better understand what is better for you. There is no right or wrong answer. Only what is the best option for you.

My favorite quote on experience:

"Experience is one thing you can't get for nothing." – Oscar Wilde

Question #5 – "Why Leave the Security of My Job?"

Growing up we have all been taught to get a good education and that will lead to a good job. Work hard in that job and good things will happen. This has worked well for many generations. In fact, for most of us starting out in life this is the best option or the only option. Unless you are born into wealth or win the lottery it takes time to accumulate the necessary capital to put you in a position to even consider starting any type of business.

I have heard countless times over my career from very successful people, "I have a great job. If I leave and start a business, then I am giving up the security of a steady paycheck." There is no arguing on this point. I will be the first to tell you that there will be a sacrifice. If you want to lose 40 pounds, is it going to fall off your body by sitting on the couch or do you have to eat better and exercise to lose the weight? I am sure you have heard the expression before "No pain. No gain."

I have worked with many people over the years that will go through extraordinary pain to have their own business. "I will eat macaroni and cheese for a year in order to make my business a success." Not sure if I am comfortable going to those extremes but admire the determination.

Let's consider another thought. The security of your job. The days of having a job for life is very limited compared to 30 or 40 years ago. The Bureau of Labor Statistics says the average length of time of a worker is 4.4 years. There are two sides to this. Some Individuals want to change jobs frequently to pursue other opportunities, while others are being let go due to the constant changes in Corporate America. More commonly, individuals who have worked for the same company for 10, 20, or 30 years are now getting their pink slips.

I can tell you that this is nothing new. I have worked with many people, over the past 20 years, between the age of 40-60, that explain they were let go so the company could bring in a younger worker or a worker that is less expensive to pay.

This is very common and is not going to change. If you have not figured it out yet, this is how Corporate America works. In fact, I have gone through this with a countless amount of people that this has happened to between 2 or 3 times in their career. In fact, this is one of the major causes that pushes people into self-employed. They are tired of not having control of their own lives.

Does this mean self-employed is the answer? Maybe. I have seen many people make bad decisions on choosing a business. They do not have enough capital to support themselves until the business can support them. They do not have the skill sets to match up with the business. I am not trying to scare you from the opportunity to open your business. Just do it for the right reasons. Take your time to do your due diligence.

To get back to the main question, I hope I have given you some things to ponder. Being self-employed for over 15 years, I will share two thoughts that drive my passion for self-employment. The first is fear. The possibility that I will have to complete my resume and ask someone for a job. The second is security. Knowing that the only person in life that can fire me is my wife.

My favorite quote on security:

"Security is mostly a superstition. It does not exist in nature, nor do the children of men experience it. Avoiding danger is no safer in the long run than outright exposure. Life is either a daring adventure or nothing. – Helen Keller

Question #6 – "I Am Not Sure If I Can Work On My Own?"

Everybody in Corporate America has a boss. Even the CEO is accountable to a Board of Directors and the Board of Directors is accountable to the shareholders. The structure of Corporate America can be a very secure environment for many people. Having other co-workers around to assist in the day to day activities, managers to give you direction when needed, a good team is essential to the success of a business.

Starting a business means leaving that controlled environment. Many of the people that I have worked with have expressed this is one of the major reasons that keeps them from going solo. It could just be a self-confidence issue but I really do not believe that is it. I attribute it to the "comfort zone". The comfort zone sounds like a safe and warm environment. Maybe it is. Most self-employed individuals I know have a comfort zone. For them, it usually is an hour, a day, maybe even a week. The comfort zone is poison. Being complacent is the sure path to a failed business.

Being a business owner is not showing up every day and working 9-5, punching out and going home. It does not mean that you have to work ridiculous hours. You need to be able to adapt to the changes. Surround yourself with a team of individuals that can help you see a different point of view.

If you decide to be an independent business owner, you will need to hire those people or build a circle of influence, a group of individuals that you can count on to give you great advice.

If you decide to pursue a franchise business, you will already have a team or circle of influence from day one. The support team from the franchise corporate office has one job. To help you be successful. They already have the system, process, and experience in a specific industry. You will not be alone but have a team to advise you, based on their experiences.

Understand that any business owner is not on their own. The successful franchise owners I know even have a circle of influence outside their business. It helps them to build relationships that may pay off in new opportunities or adding additional products or services to their business.

I have worked with many entrepreneurs that do want to work alone. They want to create everything themselves and make every single decision, not listen to their employees and just tell them what to do. You may have had a boss that is a micro manager or a control freak. I am sure you have heard them say, "No one can do it better than me! Just do it this way." In the long run, did those mangers last long in their positions? Most entrepreneurs that act the same way usually hit a ceiling of growth and limit the amount of potential for their companies.

Decide which option is best for you. I can assure you will not be on your own. You are going to work for someone else or work for yourself.

My favorite quote on work:

"If you don't build your own dreams, someone will hire you to build theirs." - Tony Gaskins

Question #7 – "Why The Lack Of Support?" The Naysayers!

I wish I had a dollar for every time individuals shared with me what people close to them have said:

- "You are crazy to start a business."
- "It is a bad time to start a business."
- "I just had a friend go out of business."
- "You have a family. Wait till your kids get older."

I could go on and on. The funniest one I ever heard was, "There is a group of the 15 richest people in the world that control all the businesses. You will end up just working for them."

In all my years in business I and have not had one of them send me a paycheck yet! If you decide to pursue self employment, expect for the naysayers to come forward. It is always crucial to have feedback from other people. Especially if they are very close and you trust them. You should always listen to someone that you trust and get their feedback.

Here is the important part: You need to separate facts from fiction.

The main reason people may be putting doubts in your mind is really to protect you. They do not want to see you get hurt. You are about to do something different and most people do not like change. Your parents, spouse or best friend never want anything bad to happen to you so sometimes they will convince you that the status quo is the best thing to do. This is completely understandable. There suggestion is coming from their love for you. It is emotion based. This is the key word, "Emotion".

The most successful business owners remove emotion from their important decisions. They do not work like a psychopath with no regard for other people's feelings. Making decisions are based on the facts and the best option for their business. Unfortunately, there are times when people's feelings will get hurt but a good leader explains why the decision has been made and why it is best for the company.

This is when the naysayers lose all their credibility in helping you make a decision that is best for you. You may be shocked to hear that other people close to you do not want you to succeed?

This does sound insane. Unfortunately, I have seen it happen many times. Most of the time it stems from jealousy. Maybe your brother does not want to hear at every Thanksgiving dinner how successful you are and he is not? Is a friend afraid you will be spending all your time on your business and not have time for them? The worst comment I have ever heard was from a spouse, "If they are successful they will divorce me for a better person."

The point is this...take what everyone else says with a grain of salt. A great suggestion once given to me was, "Has this person (giving you the advice) conducted and completed any research on your business? Do they have any experience in the business? Have they been in business for themselves? Do they know someone in the business that can help give you advice? "

Do you go to the dentist because your car is making a funny sound? Do you go to your stock broker for tips on home improvement? You are probably getting the point.

Focus 90% of your decision on the facts and results of your due diligence. The other 10% is what we call gut check time. Which means, "Do the facts make common sense and is your gut agreeing."

If the answer is yes. Then do it. If the answer is no. Then don't do it.

My favorite quotes for the naysayers:

"Don't give advice to someone unless you actually have walked in the shoes that they are about to walk in" – Ken Boyce

Question #8 – "How Do I Know This Business Is Right For Me?"

The first thing you need to figure out is what do you want the business to do for you. If you are looking to get into a business to boost your ego, then save your money. Your ego will cost you plenty. Successful business owners use their business as a vehicle to provide them with a certain type of lifestyle. Here are some of the reasons I have heard over the years. Which one applies to you?

- Create more wealth.
- Tired of having a boss and just want to get up in the morning and call my own shots.
- Can't get a job that pays me like before.
- Want a business to pass on to my kids.
- Have a business that allows me more time to do the things I want to do.

Maybe you have another reason. The most important thing is to have a reason. It is not good enough just to want to be in business.

I have spoken with thousands of business owners and how they picked their business and have heard some interesting comments.

- My best friend started the same business.
- The business was going out of business and I got it for a steal.
- I love the product or service so I bought the business.
- I turned my hobby into a business.

Are you considering a business that you have experience in? Many people want to take the experience in the industry that they have worked in and start their own business. This makes perfect sense. Why not use that experience and connections to do your own thing?

In other cases, you may have a non-compete that prevents you from starting the same type of business. This tends to be very common.

I have spoken with many others that just want to make a change and have no interest in staying in the same industry.

Here are 5 suggestions to help you focus on when evaluating your business.

- Make sure you have the skill sets to operate the business.
- Make sure you will enjoy the day to day activities.
- Make sure you have more capital than you think you need.
- Make sure you conduct a professional due diligence.
- Make sure the business can produce the income you need and want.

It is amazing to me how many people do not think of these simple, straightforward suggestions. Also, make sure you have a detailed business plan and most of all execute.

My favorite quote on making the right choices in life:

Unsuccessful people make decisions based on their current situations. Successful people make decisions based on where they want to be. - Unknown

Question #9 – Do I Have the Necessary Capital to Open a Business?

This is going to be one of the most important decisions you make before opening a business. Ever heard the expression, "Cask Flow is King."? Get used to this expression if you want to run a successful business. One of the number one reasons that businesses do not make it is underfunding which is basically running out of money before they have a chance to be successful.

The key to success is having a detailed business plan and pro forma statement that outlines exactly your projected revenues and actual expenses.

The next step is to identify exactly what financing options are available to you. There are many different types of financing options available to potential franchise owners. Let's discuss a number the options that may be available to you.

- **SBA Loans** - The Small Business Administration is a government agency that provides government-backed loans for small business owners. Many franchise companies have been pre-approved for SBA loans. This helps to fast-track loans in comparison to independent business owners. The SBA does not actually make the loans but guarantees the loans with a traditional bank. The best option is to apply for an SBA loan with the bank that is on their preferred list.

- **Franchise Funding Companies** - These are companies that are focused on providing loans and financial options to franchise companies. These companies are used to dealing with the SBA, traditional banks, and offering other options to potential and existing franchise owners. The top three companies in the franchise industry are better known as Franfund, Benetrends and Guident. Each of these companies can help you streamline the process to attain financing for your franchise.

- **Rollover For Business Start-ups (ROBS)** – this program allows you to use an existing retirement account to fund your new business without incurring any debt and the funds are 100 % tax and penalty free. The IRS allows you to use your existing 401(k) funds as long as they are not with your current employer. They must originate from a previous employer. The government looks at this program as giving you the opportunity to control your retirement fund. It is crucial to work with a professional organization that understands the ROBS program. All the franchise funding companies offer this service.

- **Other Options.** You may also consider using a home equity line or a second mortgage to finance your business. Another option is a security back loan. This is when your brokerage company gives you a loan based on securing your current securities. The benefit is you do not have to liquidate your stocks or bonds.

The key to your business success is allowing your business to succeed. You cannot always control the outcomes of your efforts. I have seen business owners exceed their projections and others who have taken longer to get the results they desire. Make sure you put together conservative and realistic expectations. Reducing the stress on results will allow your business to naturally grow. I have seen so many people have unrealistic expectations that cause them to end their business too early. Most of them never gave their business the opportunity to succeed. Do not fall into this trap.

My favorite quote on money:

"It's not how much money you make but how much money you keep, how hard it works for you and how many generations you keep it for." – Robert Kiyosaki

Question #10 – "I Hear Business Owners Pay Less Taxes. Is That True?"

If you work in Corporate America, your taxes are usually very straightforward. Most people file a 1040 form. You may have a few deductions but most workers in corporate America have very little tax write-offs that can use compared to a typical business owner.

Let's go through a few examples.

- In your current position are you able to write off your car, gas, insurance expenses to your vehicle?
- Are you able to write off your vacation as an annual shareholders meeting?
- How about computers, iPads, cell phones service for phones?

Individuals that own a business have many more tax deductions than the common person. These are all legal and allowed by the IRS. Instead of paying for items in after-tax dollars now you are paying for items in pre-tax dollars, which are saving you a significant amount of income.

You also have the ability to set up different types of self-employment retirement fund accounts. There are many different types of retirement plans for self-employed individuals. Depending on your age and how much income you need on an annual basis, you may be able to defer a significant amount of your income on an annual basis to a retirement fund.

It will be important to get in contact with a Certified Professional Accountant to understand better which type of company structure is best suited for you. We will discuss corporate structures later on.

If you plan to keep your current position in corporate America and invest in a franchise business, there are significant advantages to reducing your tax burden on your personal income.

There are franchise companies that enable you to run the franchise as a semi-absentee owner. Which means that you can hire a manager to conduct the day-to-day activities and maybe put 10 to 20 hours a week of your own time into the franchise, while still working in your current position.

This is a great option for individuals who do not want to leave their current position because they are making too much money but want to eventually transition into their own business.

The advantage from a tax perspective is that individuals who have a business that shows a paper loss in their business, can take those paper losses and apply the losses to their personal income to reduce their own personal income tax.

So the answer is that you will pay fewer taxes compared to the corporate worker. In fact, in many cases, you will end up paying far less. The government rewards entrepreneurs for creating jobs and growing the economy. Take advantage of it!

My favourite tax quote:

The American people are not undertaxed. The government in Washington is overfed. - President Ronald Reagan

Question #11 – "Do I Need Experience In The Industry?"

"Makes sense, doesn't it?" Many of you have built your career on acquiring years of experience. The general consensus is to hire the person with the greatest amount of experience. In many industries, this is very true. In the franchise world this is not always the case. Franchise companies already have a detailed business plan. They know what works but more importantly know what does not work. They are looking for franchise owners that have the necessary skill sets to run their franchise business. The franchise company will educate and train their owners in the industry.

Let's explore further with the experience of one of my clients, John.

John owns a residential maid service franchise. He offers monthly cleaning services to individual household owners. John has been in business for 5 years and in the current year grossed $1.4 million in sales. John now has a solid list of clients with repeat business. John's background was managing a staff of 30 for a large technology company. During his tenure, he spent 20 years managing projects. John's professional expertise is managing people.

John will tell you that he happened to luck out finding his business. One weekend he was bored and was searching the Internet and found an advertisement promoting "Start Your Own Business" that led him to a franchise listing site. John had considered being self-employed but never really put any serious thought or research into it. He looked at many franchise companies. He became overwhelmed with the number of companies and how to determine which companies would be best for him. He saw an advertisement on working with a franchise consultant. John called me and we built his personal franchise model.

We looked at many different franchise companies and one caught his eye. The maid service caught his eye because the company was looking for individuals with experience in managing a large staff. John went through an extensive due diligence process and a month later he was signing his franchise agreement and starting a new business.

John will tell you that never in a million years did he think that he would own a business, more so, that he would own a maid service. It took one Saturday afternoon of fortunate timing to help lead him to his current path. This is a rare occurrence for most individuals searching a business. Many will look for a business that looks sexy or relates to their personal interests. This tends to lead to investing in the wrong business and eventually dissatisfaction. They also do not have someone that understands the franchise industry who can expose them to quality companies.

It is crucial to limit your preconceptions and assumptions. Open your mind, focus on what you are good at and use those skills to your benefit.

There are plenty of great opportunities. Take your time. The right opportunity will not be difficult to finally decide on. If it is difficult to make that decision, then do not do it. Wait and find the one that does fit.

My favorite quote on experience:

"The only source of knowledge is experience." – Albert Einstein

Question #12 – Is It Wise To Have Family Members In My Business?

Having a family member as a business partner may seem like a good idea from a personal and business perspective. The truth is, it can prove challenging to work with family, especially if things do not go as planned.

Here are some questions to consider before making your family part of your day-to-day business.

- **What Happens When We Disagree?**

Disagreements with family can be difficult when personal feelings become involved based on decisions that affect the business. It is important to remain professional and focus on what is best for the business. Make up specific terms to eliminate personal feelings from those business decisions.

- **Determine Why You Are In Business Together.**

Write down why you will work well together and if you are going in the same direction. Define the goals for the business and make plans on who will make final decisions.

- **Define Your Specific Roles.**

It is crucial to define your roles and responsibilities. There has to be specific accountability when things need to be addressed in the business.

- **What Are Your Skill Sets?**

Do your skill sets compliment each other? Make sure you are not doing the same job. Divide and conquer always makes better partnerships.

- **Can You Keep Your Personal And Professional Lives Separate?**

This is difficult but necessary. The best strategy is to not discuss work at family events or after work hours. Set up a policy that is clearly defined.

- **Set Up An Evaluation Process.**

You will need to hold each other accountable and develop an evaluation process on the performance of your positions. In some situations, it may be necessary to hire an independent consultant to hold quarterly reviews.

- **Set Up A Partnership Agreement.**

Before asking a family member to become your partner, you must engage in a partnership agreement that defines duties, share of profits and an exit strategy if things do not work out.

My favorite family quote:

"The love of family and the admiration of friends is much more valuable than wealth and privilege." – Charles Kuralt

Question #13 – "Is It OK To Have A Business Partner?"

This is a very common question that stems from many reasons. Here are some of the main reasons I have heard over the years.

- **My friend and I want to start a business together.**
- **Want to reduce my risk.**
- **Want to start a business with my family.**
- **Need a financial partner to invest the money.**
- **Do not want to leave my job.**

Let's first discuss the positive aspects of having a business partner.

- **Time** – You can not be in two places at one time. Dividing the tasks of the business can enable you to grow your business larger than yourself. You can also go on vacation without having to worry about your business.

- **Trust** – Working with someone that you have known for years. This could be a co-worker, friend or family member. A business partnership is much like a marriage. Your success will depend on how you work together and depending on each other to do the right things.

- **Financial** – Sharing financial resources can be very appealing. It may be the only way to put yourself in a position to start the business or reduce your financial exposure.

- **Experience** – Starting your first business may be scary. Having someone that has already done it can provide you with more confidence.

Let's discuss the negative aspects of having a business partner.

- **Sharing Profits** – Depending on your percentage of ownership, you will now be sharing the profits. That means you will have to generate more revenue to make your needed income. The key is to make sure your business has the ability to make the revenue in order to accomplish both of your desired incomes.

- **Shared Equity** – It is important to consider your exit strategy for the business. Many people do not. Make sure you are both on the same timeline. You may want to sell the business and your business partner does not. It is crucial to have a partnership agreement that specifically addresses this and many other issues that may arise in the future.

- **Potential Loss of Relationship** – This happens many times. You may have a great relationship prior to opening your business. If your business does not meet your expectations, will it have a negative impact on your relationship? Are you willing to take that risk? Just because you have a good relationship does not mean you will work well together. Talk about those things in great detail. Make a list of defining takes and who is responsible for each aspect of the business. The more you put in writing the better.

- **Health** – Many partnerships have to end because of health issues. It is always something no one wants to happen but it often does. Make sure you both get physicals. Getting life insurance on each other is also very important. It can help reduce the risk to the business in the case of death.

These are just a few of the things to consider before determining whether a partnership is right for you. Put as many things down on paper or in your partnership agreement that protects both of you.

The best business partnerships that I have seen are when the business partners bring different skill sets to the business. One partner may excel at sales while the other is best at managing staff. In business partnerships, opposites can be a very good thing. You are focused on one key aspect of the business and your partner focuses on another. That way you are not stepping on each other's toes and you can assign defined responsibilities.

My favorite quote on partnerships:

"It is rare to find a business partner who is selfless. If you are lucky it happens once in a lifetime." – Michael Eisner

Question #14 – "How Should I Structure My Business?"

There are many different ways to structure your business. The first thing to do is find a professional to determine which structure is going to be best for you. Depending on your current situation, you may need an Attorney, a Certified Professional Accountant or both.

The main things to consider are protecting your personal assets and reducing your taxes. Everyone's situation is going to be unique. There are five main structures to consider.

- **Sole Proprietorship**

A sole proprietorship is owned by one person and there is no legal difference that separates the owner from the business. Any profit or loss flows directly to the business owner.

Advantages: Sole proprietorships are simple to open and maintain. It works very much like working for a company except that you only pay taxes on the profits from the business.

Disadvantages: The main disadvantage is not protecting your personal assets. There is no corporate structure that separates you from the company.

- **Partnership**

A partnership is usually two individuals but can be more. There can also be a difference in the percentage of ownership and share of profits.

Advantages: You don't have to register with the state or incur fees to start a partnership. The earnings are also split and taxed in the personal names of the partners.

Disadvantages: Just like a sole proprietorship, the partner's personal assets are not protected by the company. Splitting the profits can also reduce your rate of returning your investment.

- **Corporations**

Corporations are the most common structure. The corporation is given legal rights and separates the owners from the company. Corporations are owned by shareholders and the shareholder's personal assets cannot be put at risk from a lawsuit to the corporation.

Advantages: The limited liability of a corporation protects its owners from lawsuits and debts. The corporation is taxed separately. The owners only pay taxes on salaries, bonuses and dividends.

Disadvantages: There are registration fees and paperwork that must be submitted to the government. Corporations may be taxed twice, on the profits and again on dividends paid to shareholders.

- **S Corporation**

An S Corporation is a type of corporation but does not typically pay income taxes. The profits are passed on to the owners of the shareholders. It still has the same advantage of a corporation with the protection for the shareholders.

Advantages: Shareholders have limited personal liability as with a corporation.

Disadvantages: S Corporations typically have more regulations to maintain and are usually costly to set up.

- **Limited Liability Company (LLC)**

A Limited Liability Company (LLC) combines a sole proprietorship with a corporation. Similar to a corporation the owners have limited liability and separate their personal assets. The profits of the LLC are passed through as income to the owners.

Advantages: The LLC has options that allow owners to be taxed as a corporation, sole proprietor, partnership or S corporation.

Disadvantages: Unless you choose to be taxed as a corporation, LLCs are usually subject to self-employment taxes. This means that the profits of the LLC will not be taxed at the corporate level, but will pass through to its members who will account for those profits on their personal federal tax returns.

My Favorite Quote on Structure:

"**Unless structure follows strategy, inefficiency results.**" - **Alfred Chandler**

Question #15 – "Is Owning A Business Better Than Working In Corporate America?"

Is owning a business better than working in a job? Yes, maybe and no. I am not trying to confuse you. It really depends on what works for you.

- Are you interested in making more money?
- Looking for more time to spend with your family?
- Want to call your own shots?

You may have similar reasons of your own. I have heard many different reasons, having spoken with thousands of business owners. May I suggest a different thought?

"Will owning a business make you happier?"

Most business owners start a business because they are unhappy with their current job or lifestyle. They have an existing source of pain that they want to eliminate or a desire they wish to fulfill. Owning a business does not mean you will not have to work anymore. You still need to get up every morning and go to work in your business. You will have good days and bad days, just like your current job. So why?

The best reason I ever heard from a business owner was, "The only person that is going to fire me now is my spouse!"

Have you had a boss that you did not like or a company that is making decisions that affect the outcome of your life? Most business owners that I have met are much happier than people I know that work in Corporate America. Why is that? I searched out for an answer. I spoke with many of my friends that work in Corporate America and asked them for the top 3 issues or challenges they are experiencing. The results were very interesting.

- **Limited Income** – the average salary for the corporate worker has been stagnant over the past 10 years. This is by far the number one concern. There is tremendous frustration on not being able to get ahead.

- **Working More Hours** – I personally love the new technology available to me that enables me to control my life. The smart phone for me has been the best invention ever. I can control when and how to work in my business. This is not the feedback I heard from most corporate workers. Most people felt that they were "On Call" because of the instant accessibility of todays technology and their companies looked down on them if they did not work more hours than their counterparts.

- **Unsecured Future** – Have you ever been "downsized" or let's just say what it is "fired". In the past, most people were fired because they did not do their job well. Not today. Corporate America decides to eliminate a division and you are out of a job. This is very much the commonplace today.

The common thread to business ownership is control. Business owners are dictating the path to their future. Each decision made has a consequence. If you are making the right decisions currently in Corporate America, why not make those decisions in your own business?

My favorite Corporate America Quote:

"I always like to refer managers of Corporate America as the renters of the corporate assets, not the owners." – Henry Kravis

Question #16 – "Which Industries Have the Best Opportunity?"

This is one of most common questions that people ask. It may be asked in other terms:

- What is a hot industry?
- I heard this industry is exploding?
- This industry looks exciting.
- Top 10 businesses to open.

Do not get caught up in the hype of opening a business in a particular industry. There are many paid advertisements promoting industries that may not be the right time to open. Be careful and do your proper research.

A very common statement that I have heard is "These locations are popping up everywhere!"

Timing is important but not everything. There are industries that become obsolete. Does anyone today sell VCR's? There is a life cycle to every business. The life cycle of a business has 5 stages.

- Start-Up
- Growth
- Maturity
- Decline
- Death

Choosing the stage of your business will depend on your risk tolerance. Is there an advantage to be first with a product or service? Is being an innovator worth the risk? Maybe it is wise to pause and learn from the experiences of the initial company to the industry? You need to consider the risks and rewards on entry into an industry. A pioneer will take a larger risk developing market awareness. A late market entry will need to develop strategies to differentiate their product or service.

Being the first company in an industry may provide a considerable advantage but it will cost you more to learn what works and does not work. Many companies like to enter into a market second or third and learn from the pioneer, reducing the risk and learning curve to compete. Pioneers can definitely become the giant in the industry but many times a competitor can pivot easier and take significant market share. Taking advantage of weaknesses and finding unique options to offer their product or service.

In my opinion, being a pioneer creates too much risk for most individuals who cannot afford to make the mistakes that cost them considerable time and capital. Entering a market that has been established will be far less risk. You just need to make sure that you provide a comparable or superior product or service. Entering into a franchise system can reduce the time and risk of entering a market and also opening the doors to industries that require you to have no experience.

Determining your risk tolerance and capital flexibility will help determine the proper path for your first business.

My favorite quote on timing:

"Don't wait for the perfect moment, take the moment and make it perfect." – Unknown

Question #17 – "Should I Purchase An Existing or Start-up Business?"

The decision to buy an existing business or start a new one depends on many factors.

- Available capital.
- Need to generate income.
- Time available to participate in the business.

Start-up companies always experience growing pains and usually take longer to become successful. The flip side is starting a company and seeing it grow can be very rewarding.

Purchasing an existing business eliminates the necessary time to develop the company into an ongoing entity. The flip side is you are inheriting existing employees and systems that may not agree with you.

There are positive and negatives to both options.

When financing a business, you will find that an existing business will be easier to finance than a start-up. An existing business will have history and current income. A start-up will be more difficult to finance due to the lack of history and income. The difference will be the investment level. Typically, an existing business will cost much more than a start-up company. You will be paying a premium for the work that already has been completed.

Start-up companies are far riskier than a proven business. Investment firms expect there will be more failures and less positive results with start-ups. Start-up business owners will deal with learning their business, being accepted by the marketplace and the ability to show a profit. An existing business already has customers, revenue, and proven success.

When you are ready or purchase a business, you will need to review the financial statements and what the company is worth. Financial statements will not always be accurate and need to be reviewed by a financial professional. You will also need to evaluate the current employee structure and whether they want to work for you.

When you buy an existing business the benefit starts immediately because the company is already generating revenue and is making a profit. Start-up companies go through a period of time where they typically do not make any profit. The benefit is less initial investment and a better return on investment. You also have a fresh canvas to build your business.

The benefit of purchasing a franchise is you get the best of both worlds. You buy into a proven business model but have a start-up company to paint your business your way with the guidance the franchisor. In some cases, you may be able to purchase an existing franchise location that has already been established. The key difference is a franchisee must report its financial statements to the franchisor making the accuracy of the evaluation far more accurate.

My favorite decision quote:

"Unsuccessful people make decisions based on their current situation, successful people make their decisions based on where they want to be." - Unknown

Question #18 – "How Do I Perform Due Diligence On A Business?"

The key to opening a successful business starts with the due diligence. Due diligence is the process of reviewing all of the available documentation related to that business. The goal is to review and analyze all legal and financials relating to the business and determine if the business will accomplish your personal and financial goals. It is crucial to make sure there are no surprises that you may pay for after the purchase of your business.

Due diligence demands that you to conduct a proper venting process. You will need the assistance of a financing company, accountant, and attorney to help you complete your due diligence.

The due diligence process may be different depending on the age of the business. The following is a framework to help cover the main criteria:

- **Financials.** Getting audited financial statements is critical. You probably have heard the term "cooking the books", financial statements that are not representative of the financial position of the company. Ask for balance sheets, income statements and tax returns for the past five years. Have an accountant review the documents and ask these questions.

- **Legal issues.** Hiring a business or franchise attorney is required. You need to review any copies of the business' agreements, proprietary property, customer contracts, and licenses. Make sure the company is not under any direct lawsuits that may have an effect on your business. You may have the current owner stay on for a transitional period. Make sure this is defined in an agreement.

- **Employees.** Define and review organizational charts, employment agreements, benefits plan, non-compete and confidentiality agreements. Most times the business owner will not want you to speak with current employees because they do not want to upset them with a change. Many times requesting a meeting with key employees before a final transaction can be arranged.

- **Customers or Clients.** Understand the current relationships with customers or clients. Will they continue to be customers if you purchase the business? You need to expect to lose customers. It will be difficult to know the exact percentage but the norm tends to be 10-15%. Meeting with the current VP of Sales or Sales Manager can give you a good indication of the state of the customer relations.

- **Vendors.** Request a list of suppliers and vendors. Understand the current contracts or commitments to those current suppliers and vendors. Researching alternative options is good to see if the current companies are offering reasonable pricing.

- **Franchises.** Most individuals that purchase a franchise business are opening a start-up business. They do not have any previous results to base their research. You need to work with the franchise company to educate you on the due diligence process. The key is to validate all the information with the current franchisees.

Once you complete your due diligence process, you will have all the information to understand if the business meets your necessary requirements and verify the pricing of the business.

Favorite due diligence quote:

"Finding out the truth is half of it. It's what you do with it what matters." – Tristan Wilds

Question #19 – "How Long Will It Take To Make Money?"

How long will it take for my business to become profitable? The most important question a potential business owner should ask. Most business owners leave Corporate America with senior positions looking forward to taking their future into their own hands. Replacing that income is the largest concern most people have and want to know when their investment will pay off. The answer is not always clear-cut.

Businesses have many different time frames to profitability. For example, home-office, low investment businesses will likely become profitable faster than storefront businesses because they have fewer opening and operating expenses. It is important to understand the specific amount of income you need to make and eventually want to make. There are businesses considered to be "buy a job" business where the ceiling of potential is limited. These businesses tend to be lower investment and single owner operated with no employees. If you are looking for significantly more income, investing in a business with employees and multiple locations will be a better fit.

Before talking about profitability, let's understand how to determine profit. The simple definition of profit is revenue minus expenses equals profit. It is important to determine what profit you need before choosing your business. Are you interested in just "paying the bills" or "accumulating wealth"? It is crucial to build a personal wealth plan if you decide on business ownership. You will not have corporate benefits or 401k plans that are provided by Corporate America. Treat your business as a vehicle that is driving you to your destination. You need to have a financial GPS and how many miles it will take you to reach your destination.

Most business owners finance all or a portion of their initial investment.

Acquiring a business loan requires the borrower to submit financial projections that estimate the profitability of the business. Here are items that you need to be considering.

- **Break-Even Point.** There are two types of break-even points. Cash flow break-even and initial investment break-even. Cash flow break-even is your revenue minus your operating expenses. Initial investment break-even adds the amount of your initial investment to your operating expenses. This may be your loan payment or amortizing your initial cash investment over a period of time. Many people make the mistake of not differentiating the two. It is important to understand that you will be able to use the profit you make in the business to pay off your initial investment. This profit is usually free of tax until your initial investment is paid back. A Certified Professional Accountant will be able to help you evaluate the tax implications.

The next step is to determine potential long-term revenue by preparing a pro forma income statement.

- **Sales Projections.** You need to make educated estimates on sales in your business for at least the next one to three years. It is important to make three projections. An aggressive, moderate and conservative projection.

- **Cost of Goods Sold.** Whether you are selling a product or service, you will need to create a cost of goods sold budget report. This report will help you to create a more accurate forecast.

- **Fixed Expenses.** Determine the cost of your fixed expenses such as rent, phone, internet, accounting, marketing, insurance, utilities, salaries, and debt repayments.

- **Gross Profit.** You have the information to determine the range of potential profit. Take your sales projections, deduct your cost of goods sold and fixed expenses to estimate your gross profit.

A great resource to use is the Small Business Administration. The have tools and resources to assist you at www.sba.gov.

My favorite assumptions quote:

"People do not want to hear the truth because they don't want their illusions destroyed." – Friedrich Neitz

Question #20 – Use Retirement Funds To Fund A Business?

Most people are not aware that they are able to use retirement funds to purchase a business. The IRS allows you to transfer funds from your retirement to purchase a business without penalty or having to include those funds as income for the current year. We discussed earlier but let's get into more detail.

The ROBS (Rollover For Business Start-Ups) allows you to transfer money from an eligible retirement account, such as a 401(k) or traditional IRA, and invest it in your business without paying income taxes or early withdrawal penalties. A ROBS program is not a loan, you are not required to pay back the amount removed to your retirement account. It is crucial to work with a company that focuses on the ROBS program. Here are the basic steps:

- Step 1 – Form A C Corporation.
- Step 2 – Create a 401(k) plan for the corporation.
- Step 3 – Transfer funds from your personal retirement account.
- Step 4 – The plan uses the funds to purchase stock in the company.
- Step 5 – Proceeds from the sale of the stock are used to purchase the business.

The first thing is you need to identify is if your funds qualify. Working with one of the professional groups, we discussed earlier, will be able to help you determine if your funds are accessible.

There are two points of view on whether to use retirement funds for a business. The first is not to touch your retirements until retirement. The other point of view is it is better for you to take control of your own money instead of having Wall Street try and make you money. I believe there is truth in both points of view.

Here are some of the pros and cons of the ROBS program.

PROS

- **No debt or interest payments.** Since you are using your own money there is no need to acquire capital and the interest expense for a new business or to buy an existing business. That means the business is cash rich and provides more flexibility.

- **Greater Success Rates** – ROBS program businesses have a higher success rate due to less debt and more cash. Putting less stress on the business creates a better opportunity for its success.

- **No income taxes or early withdrawal penalties.** This is one of the major reasons people use the ROBS program. It is far cheaper than raising traditional debt financing or having a business partner.

- **Personal credit is not affected.** The ROBS requires no credit check which opens up more options if you require additional financing.

- **Growth of retirement funds.** Under a ROBS program, a 401(k) plan is created for the company. You can contribute to that account as your business produces revenue and use the funds for retirement.

CONS

- **Possible business failure.** Starting a business is about taking control of your life and making money for your family. There is always the chance you will not be successful. If so, you will not be responsible to pay back your 401(k). It will be the same as losing stock value.

- **Audit from IRS.** The IRS allows the ROBS program as long as the program is set up correctly. That is why it is important to hire a professional to make sure the program is set up according to IRS rules. There are no issues as long as you do not try to cut corners and submit the proper paperwork to the IRS. The IRS is only concerned with abusers of the program who are not operating an ongoing business.

- **Need to have a plan administrator.** With the ROBS program, you become a company retirement plan and need an administrator. That can be you or hire a company to assist. It's only possible to do a ROBS if you're structured as a C Corporation. The simplicity and tax advantages of an LLC are preferable but you are giving that up if you decide to do a ROBS program.

It is crucial to use the guidance of a professional ROBS firm.

My favorite quote on following what everyone else does:

"Following what everyone else is doing is rarely a way to get rich." – Jim Rogers.

www.ingramcontent.com/pod-product-compliance
Lightning Source LLC
Chambersburg PA
CBHW070409190526
45169CB00003B/1183